Sunstars in the Meltswamp

Marion Frahm Tincknell

FIVE RIVERS PRESS
SAGINAW, MICHIGAN

Copyright © 2015 Marion Frahm Tincknell
All rights reserved.
ISBN: 0692236058
ISBN-13: 978-0692236055

To the many people I love, and have loved, most especially my very patient, encouraging husband, Les.

CONTENTS

ACKNOWLEDGMENTS IV
INTRODUCTION V
A POTENTIALLY POETIC PLACE 1
    GREENPOINT IN MARCH 2
    EARLY, EARLY SPRING 3
    VIOLETS AND RAIN 4
    JUST DAWN 5
    SUMMER HEAT 6
    SOUNDS OF SUMMER REMEMBERED 8
    GULF WIND 9
    OCEAN 10
    LANDSCAPE 11
    ROCKY MOUNTAIN TIME 12
    REDWOODS 13
    CLOUD 14
    UNBEAUTIFUL 15
    END OF SUMMER 16
    OCTOBER IN THE WOODS 17
    THE BRINK WINTER 18
    WINTER BEACH 19
    OUTDOORS 20
THE WALLS WHISPER OUR SECRETS 21
    ROOMS 22
    HEARTHSIDE 23
    NEW MILFORD DEPOT, 1939 24
    THANKSGIVING AT NANNY'S 25
    FATHER, IN MEMORIAM 26
    THE BLUE SPRUCE CAFE 27
    FLAT TIRE, FLUSHING, L.I. (circa 1909) 28
    1944 29
    BABS - 1947 30
    WHAT I WISH I'D KNOWN ABOUT THE PROM 31
    MOVING - April 1965 32
    MUSEUM ART CLASS 33
    BEACH WONDERS 34
    THE RITUAL 35
    DAUGHTER / DAUGHTER 36
    QUIET ROOMS 37
    BRET ANDREW, February 5, 2003 38
    PREPARING THE HOLE 39

THE WINDING TRAIL OF EXPLORERS' DREAMS 41
- UNWINDING 42
- ART EXHIBIT 43
- WASHINGTON METRO 44
- CHICAGO IN SUMMER 45
- CITY SUMMER NIGHT 46
- VICKSBURG 47
- GRAND CANYON 48
- HIGHWAY CALIFORNIA 49
- DENALI / McKINLEY 50
- PYRAMIDS OF TEOTiHUACAN 51
- OAXACANA 52
- CATHEDRAL CONCERT, OAXACA 53
- FRANCE - AFTER ALL THESE YEARS 54
- THE STREETS OF ROUEN 55
- THE BELLS OF NURNBURG 56
- GOURNIA, CRETE 57
- VENICE IN OCTOBER 58
- WHITE NIGHT, FINLAND 60
- GUILIN, CHINA 61
- ANCIENT CITY, SUZHOU 62

RAINBOWS FROM MY PRISMS 63
- MY FRIEND / MY LOVER / MY CHILD 64
- FRIENDSHIP 65
- A LOVE POEM 66
- VOWS 67
- THE WEDDING POEM 68
- LITTLE BRACELETS OF FLAME 69
- LOVE SEASONS 70
- THE GOLDEN CIRCLE 71
- COMFORT 72
- THE TOY SHOP 73
- RENDEZVOUS 74
- JUST DESSERT 75
- GODIVA'S SECRET 76

SECRETS THEY DO NOT SHARE 77
- "ALL THE MONKEYS AREN'T IN THE ZOO" 78
- LEOPARD 79
- NICHOLAS 80
- PUSSY CAT, PUSSY CAT, WHERE HAVE YOU BEEN? 81
- HAYLEY IN MIDDLE AGE 82
- MIGRATION NORTH 83
- SEA GULL 84

SEAGULL SYMPHONY	85
PIGEONS	86
MALLARD	87
THE MAGICAL SHIMMER	**89**
THE QUEEN REFLECTS	90
THE SLEEPING BEAUTY	91
GLASS SHOES	92
THE LEGEND OF KYLA, HAWK WOMAN	94
THE LADY OF SHALOTT	96
PUTTING ON BILLY COLLINS' CLOTHES	97
SHADOW IN THE GLASS HOUSE	98
FREIGHT TRAIN	99
BRASSY RHYTHM	100
ALL THINGS CONSIDERED	**101**
TESTING THE OPTIONS	102
ANGELS	103
MODERN ANGELS	104
UNFORGIVEN	105
ALL WHO EVER LIVED	106
SEPTEMBER 10, 2003	108
UNCONDITIONAL	109
PROBLEMS BEING ACCEPTED	**111**
BREAKING BARRIERS	112
WINNIE	113
PORTRAIT OF A MARRIAGE	114
FIRST LADY	115
JARED'S MOTHER	116
MARILYN / NORMA JEAN – 1996	117
GUEST POET	118
I WISH YOU CHRISTMAS	**119**
CHURCH WINDOWS	120
THE INNKEEPER'S GRANDDAUGHTER	121
PERILOUS JOURNEY	122
THE CHILD	124
FORGOTTEN FATHER	125
A GRANDMOTHER'S MEDITATION	126
LEAH'S CHRISTMAS	128
CHRISTMAS WISHES	129
PUBLISHING CREDITS AND AWARDS	**131**
ABOUT THE AUTHOR	**136**

ACKNOWLEDGMENTS

Deep appreciation to my husband,
Leslie D. Tincknell,
for his generosity, persistence, and encouragement
in the production of this book.

Many thanks to Maxine Harris and Betty Van Ochten
for their valuable editing, critique, and encouragement.

Especial appreciation to my son, Paul, for generously devoting his time,
expertise, and artistry to the creation of this book.

COVER ILLUSTRATION

Sunstars in the Meltswamp
by
Leslie D. Tincknell

INTRODUCTION

Inspired by sunlight flashing in the puddles surrounding the trees, the opening poem, *Greenpoint in March*, refers to "sunstars in the meltswamp." I am hoping that readers will find sunstars flashing amid the morass of words in the poems that follow.

Every work of art requires two artists: the creator and the viewer/reader. Without a reader, my poems do not exist. Please read and bring YOUR art to my words. My words may surprise you; your interpretation surely would surprise me! Read on ... let's create together.

~*Marion F. Tincknell*

A POTENTIALLY POETIC PLACE

GREENPOINT IN MARCH

Sunstars sparkle in the meltswamp
where ice wafers float around the trees.
Slender green threads, lured by sudden heat,
struggle out of the leaf-soup,
and a frog sits on the path,
unsure why he awakened so early.

Birds sing atop the bony trees,
unaware that winter, still snapping her teeth,
has a nasty snarl ready for tomorrow.

The woods, winter-tangled and needing combing,
await slow greening
where sunstars sparkle among the ice wafers
melting around their chilly knees.

EARLY, EARLY SPRING

A bedraggled witch leans against a porch pillar,
staring down on shivering crocuses.
Across the street,
a desperate Christmas wreath,
red bow askew,
sprinkles brown confetti on the doorstep.

A pumpkin leafbag slumps under the bushes
of a neighbor's house.
Here and there,
despondent Santas sag against chimneys
or roof gables,

as a pink balloon bunny
bobs beside the porch steps,
and the hedge around the corner is polka-dotted
with a bushel of plastic eggs.

When evening deepens to dark,
holiday candles come to life in windows,
and lighted icicles drip from the eaves

even as willows swing yellowing fronds
in the biting wind
and forsythia draws breath for flowers.

VIOLETS AND RAIN

The empty lot was all
tall trees and violets,
a million miles from the city street
that passed along one edge.
A footpath cut diagonally across,
a shortcut from the bus stop.

We picked violets –
bunches and bunches.
fragile stems,
tiny flowers.

One spring day, it rained ...
rained in columns.
We stood in patches of sunlight between
columns of rain,
violets showering around our feet.

JUST DAWN

In blackest silence of the night,
birds murmur
and fling their songs at thick absorbent dawn.

What thinning of the night
drains their sleep away?

A distant rooster bells his cry into a tissue sky,
a sky so sheer
the next shrill call tears a rent the sun bleeds through.

Winds hang lightly in the trees,
brush-blending new scarlet up the curving sky.
The birds gulp light ...
and sing!

SUMMER HEAT

1
The boat cruises in a following wind.
Dozing in blazing sun,
a young woman lies on the cabin roof,
blanketed with heat.

2
The children race along the beach,
laughing,
pails swinging, ready for treasures.
Their feet dance on the searing sand.

3
Heat shimmers along dark pavement,
sluices down the glass-and-concrete canyons,
wavers in cocoons around buses and cars,
withers the parched grass on park floors.
Wilted pedestrians steam in the crossings,
tempers primed for the match!

4
Hikers stride into the woods,
tightwalk the stones in a stream, begin to climb.
Insects hum.
Their packs weigh heavier,
shirts soaked on their backs.
Dust puffs in plumes under foot.
Knees melt and muscles burn;
rocks and roots litter the path.
The sun relentless, they toil to the turn,
strain up and up.
At last, packs shrugged off,
boots unlaced,
they share a canteen of warm water.

5
No breeze lifts the curtains to freshen twisted sheets.
Tendrils of damp hair tangle on the pillow.
They kiss and
roll apart.
Too hot!

6
The roller coaster tick-tick-ticks
and rumbles down the steep track.
A calliope waltzes with children and horses.
Tiny airplanes race in rattling circles.
A soup of sweat, rancid grease, and redpop simmers
in a cauldron of amusements,
boils in the sunny glare,
melting snowcones and poison-pink cotton candy.

7
Heat lightning finger-paints the clouds
at the edge of day and night.
One star tests the eastern dark.
Families sprawl on blankets, grandmas on folding chairs.
Kids swing spitting sparklers, space ships
from the stars.
A long whistle and boom of thunder -
a burst of red and gold and glitter
blooms into a giant chrysanthemum
and rains magic.
Heat soothes into cooling air
as the summer night explodes in color and sound,
blue fountains,
golden waterfalls,
ribbons of stars -
and lightning etching clouds along the horizon.

SOUNDS OF SUMMER REMEMBERED

I remember,
spinning through the morning haze into my summer dream,
the whr-r whr-r of a boy-power mower,
the twang-ng-bang! of the back-door screen.

A distant radio murmur blends into sounds
of surf disintegrating on the sand it pounds.

I hear the silence of a lake at twilight,
gleaming,
stitched by the puttery-putt of an outboard
across the melon-soft evening,
the buzzz-alarm of locusts warning of August heat,
the night-time rasp that katydids monotonously beat.

Mist in the morning and rain at noon,
I listen at the window in wonder,
rain pattering gently into sodden leaves
and distant rumbling thunder.

Sometimes now, in a sudden silence,
I hear summer once again -
a katydid somewhere,
or locusts,
and always in a gentle rain.

GULF WIND

A ceaseless wind weaves through stiff grass
stitched tightly to the sand.
Gulls swoop and glide
astride air stallions plunging above the dunes and waves.
Combing through wiry weeds,
the incessant winds whisk feathers of sand into fluid sculptures.
As wind and water mold the beach,
treasures rise and disappear.

The wind reshapes the wanderer
who scavenges the shore.
In his hoard of shells and scoured skeletons,
he will find wind-wound thoughts for winter nights.

OCEAN

The ocean goes on being beautiful -
and terrible – day after day
making lace on the shore
with rolling fingers,
pounding ancient cliffs
with ferocious fists.

Its grey, mournful, heaving beauty
glitters, frothy and silky,
with silver sequins.

The sea tosses treasure on its beaches –
stars and bones, shells and stones –
enticing divers into its green depths
in search of more.

It lures adventurers and mercenaries
to try its surface ...
brings them home –
or not.

Is that singing in the waves
music
or mockery?

LANDSCAPE

We walk the shadowed path beside a lake,
wind-ruffled above reflections of snow-crowned peaks.
A mallard cruises parallel to the shore,
pretending that we are not there.
We stop in the wavering light,
watching.

The path winds away from the lake,
leads us down to a cascade, frothing
over polished stones and gleaming logs.
Chilled air sweeps down the ravine,
a message from the glacier, hanging
on the mountain above.

Two chipmunks chase each other
along a fallen tree;
one dives into a cave of roots.
The other stands upright, eight inches
from our feet,
then dashes away among the giant jackstraws
littering the forest floor.

Around the curve of the lake,
cattails bend to sun and wind.
Trees, crowding the shore,
have lost their footing and fallen
head first into the water.
Saplings grow upright from their trunks,
a new forest reborn.

ROCKY MOUNTAIN TIME

I stand upon a slide of rock,
whitewater roaring at my feet, and
look through spire upon spire of spruce and pine and fir
upon pinnacles of stone and ice.

It challenges comprehension to consider
the epochs of creation
that have heaved up these mountains
and the forces of wind and water spent
upon refining their form.

There are merely centuries in the evergreen forests,
a few years in the aspen groves,
and a moment am I,
observing eons backward
and beauty outward...
> the torrent incessant at my feet,
> the wind never silent in my hair,
> the roots of the forest and lichen on the rocks,
> all
> imposing change by moment and hour
> into eras yet to come.

REDWOODS

Their heads swathed in clouds,
they rise inch by inch,
millennium after millennium,
whispering to the winds
and casting deep shadows
over ferns crowding their feet.

Seedlings shouldered out of the loam
as Phoenicians dipped their oars
into the Mediterranean
and grew knee high as Roman centurions
stamped into Jerusalem.

At shoulder height, they
trembled while Normans advanced
upon the Saxons, then stretched taller
as Marie Antoinette's head rolled
into a basket.

As they heightened century upon century,
Japanese composed ethereal haiku
even as they wrought Samurai havoc
among helpless peasants,
Wordsworth praised golden daffodils,
and Wagner's chords pounded
the gates of Valhalla.

As the world below
steals and bullies and destroys,
sings and dances, sculpts and builds,
the redwoods inch higher
and watch.

CLOUD

One cloud, painting the color of stone
over the dome of the sky,
mutes autumn gold.

The lake is steel-colored glass
without a ripple disturbing burnt umber
in its upside-down world.

Fog feathers quiver at the feet
of trees standing in pools
of caramel leaves.

The cloud drops a veil of mist,
blurs the woods and meadows,
drizzles cold misery into rivers,

and drums silver rain
onto rocks and cornfields, roofs
and cattle huddled at the barnyard gate.

The air chills.
Storing snow in its pockets,
the great cloud broods.

UNBEAUTIFUL

Grey rags hang from the sky
to the ridge of distant mountains.
A gauze of mist veils the window.
Like tiny balloons, bubbles float on the walk.

We slog into the raw rain,
water sluicing from our umbrella,
slopping the hems of our pants,
and slosh into the Flying Goat.

Steaming lattes between us,
we read and talk, watch rain
cascading from the awning over the door.

Beautiful.

END OF SUMMER

It's not something I notice right away...
overhanging the road, a frond of red leaves
I pass under and, startled,
look back,
unbelieving.

Then a bright blue day,
all day,
crisp as apples right off the tree,
sends me back in the house for a sweater.

But the next day
shimmers in midsummer heat, clouds
rumble on the horizon, and locusts
buzz in the still afternoon.
I set a supper of sliced peaches and sweet corn
in the shade as
the evening sky turns to purple,
and flames.

Plans begin for fall meetings and,
on an excursion to the stores for summer shirts,
I see the display designer setting out
pumpkins, witches, and ghosts.

OCTOBER IN THE WOODS

A leaf fell in the silent golden woods.
Tongues of autumn fire have licked summer from the trees
        now ankle deep in pools of tawny color—
              butterscotch and umber,
              cinnamon and copper.

A leaf fell in the silent golden woods.
The wintry wind weaves strands of snow
              into the loom of trees.
A silent music sounds from rustled leaves,
              from the cascade of an icy stream.

A leaf fell -
a minute of forest time
falling in the silent golden woods.

THE BRINK WINTER

The trees are standing in their bones,
cold,
the death breath of winter
whistling through their stretched fingers.

Late fall has become as pale as early spring
but dried and brittle.

Only chrysanthemums seem not to know
that, one night soon,
winter will stalk the garden
and bite off their pretty heads
with icy teeth.

WINTER BEACH

Life keeps close and still on the bleak beach
where an icy wind sweeps,
      ruffling no sand feathers,
      nudging no birds to fly.

Stones gleam like scattered ice cubes
in watery sunlight filtering through heavy clouds
      along the faded horizon
      where no ships sail.

Joyless water creeps up on the sand,
slides back beneath itself, and creeps up again,
      silvering a path where booted footsteps
      disappear into tightly-tied brown grasses.

Is that an echo on the frigid wind of seagull cries?
Is there a memory in murmuring water of summer songs?
      The bitter wind strums a mournful tune
      among skeleton weeds and skitters upon steel water.

OUTDOORS

The outdoors is a potentially poetic place
that only occasionally realizes its potential.
All that rhapsodizing about
purple mountains, glittering streams,
whispering winds, and cool forests!

Consider that, most of the time,
it is too hot, too cold, too wet, too snowy,
or there are too many mosquitoes
for anyone to be happy out there.
Does anyone choose to shiver, sweat, or itch?

Whatever you decide to do
to enjoy all that quivering loveliness
requires incalculable straining of muscles
to walk, climb, pedal, or row
in order to transport your protesting body
to the center of light and silence.

There you sit in the middle
of the watery, windy, wonderful wilderness
breathing scintillating, intoxicating sun and air.

Sometimes,
it's worth it!

THE WALLS WHISPER OUR SECRETS

ROOMS

Do the ghosts of those still living
haunt the rooms of childhood homes?

I walk among the rooms where I grew up
and meet my mother, young and busy,
my brothers, little boys with trains and crayons,
my father, reading the news in his wing-back chair.

Is there a hint of the icy winter day
when the furnace died?
We were bundled from our beds
to a roaring fire in the living room,
doors and windows hung with blankets
to keep away the chilling drafts.
The walls echo the anguish of Tchaikovsky
when I listened long into the nights,
lights turned low.

The young daughter sleeping in my room
sees, in her dream,
my grandma's afghan covering my bed.
I languished there, weak with flu,
uninterested in all but the bright crocheted colors.
I escaped to that room - the walls know! -
and wrote and read and dreamed.

Is there a ghostly little dog, tail flapping on the floor,
curled on the mat by the kitchen door?
We crowd the table in the dining room
with those there now
who sense our Christmases, our tree in the sunroom,
and grandparents, aunts, uncles, cousins,
all gathered for our holiday feast.

Our ghosts move among the rooms,
reflecting in the windows,
where the walls whisper our secrets.

HEARTHSIDE

The braided colors spiral around and around,
spilling into the center of the rug by the stone hearth.
Three children sit cross-legged, playing
their own game, finding
"your shirt," "my pajamas," "Bobby's bathrobe"
among the fabric patterns.
Fire fingers snap along the log
flaring behind the fire screen.
Shadows dance on the walls
as twilight deepens on the rumpled lake
beyond window and trees.
A chill wind loosens brittle leaves,
scatters them on the stony hillside.

The children set a game board
in the middle of the bright swirl of colors,
while Grandma braids old shirts and aprons
into another rug.
Mom knits a sweater
as Dad reads by lamplight in the darkening room,
flames crackling and dancing in their stone cave.
The children move game pieces
around and around the square board
in the center
of the oval rug.

NEW MILFORD DEPOT, 1939

-Train's coming!
We raced each other down the street to the station.
The snorting dragon rumbled to a stop,
steam hissing around its wheels,
hot metal ticking, ticking.
From the street-crossing, we stared,
the hulk towering above us,
breathing.

Passengers paused on the high step to look for relatives.
We were expecting Gramp
and skipping, jumping, trying to be first to see.
Greetings and laughter rang above the confusion
as bags were handed down.
The bratty boys hopped underfoot and
climbed over the baggage carts.

-A-aw - a - bo - oard!
A latecomer jumped for the last car
as the wheels screeched, began their ponderous turns.
The engine shrieked,
ripped the sizzling August afternoon,
chugged relentlessly, gathering momentum
as it thundered toward The City.

As the crowd moved away,
we grabbed Gramp's hands to drag him up the street
to the ice cream shop for purple popsicles.
Sticky ice drizzled over our fists
as the train growled,
grumbled
down the valley.

THANKSGIVING AT NANNY'S

       -She doesn't eat peas! You know,
        the tough little skins.
Aunt Evelyn, divorced and living with her parents,
primped the bow on my cousin's dress,
smoothed her hair.
Phyllis squirmed away from the fussing.
My brother decided he didn't like peas.
My mother frowned at her plate.

Nanny, still in her apron,
picked up the gravy boat and went to the kitchen.
My father growled,
       -For heaven's sake! Sit down and eat your dinner!
Nanny returned with more gravy,
an extra bowl of mashed potatoes.
       -Has everyone had cranberries?

Afterward, the family crowded in the living room,
our precious little cousin played the piano,
her mother prompting, Nanny beaming,
Gramp sucking his pipe.
My two brothers crawled behind the sofa,
shooting their fingers at each other,
shushed by Mom.
I was "old enough to know better!"
My father had "gone for a walk."

Phyllis, excused from the piano,
dragged me upstairs to look at her dolls
while the old folks dug in for talk.
Her room was perfect, the dolls
in crisp, ironed dresses, arranged
just so.
We didn't play with them.

At the door, the grown-ups laughed
and said polite thank-yous. Mother said,
     -We'll have Christmas at our house.

FATHER, IN MEMORIAM
Gustav P. Frahm, February 8, 1897 – September 20, 1962

You meet me in unexpected places.
Unannounced, you are there,
gradually lengthening your stride,
challenging me to keep pace.
I even turn my toes out to match your gait!

Your spirit sails down amidst matchless mountains
and settles beside me where I stand
swallowing the bitter pine-spiced air.

And homecomings!
I round my children in greedy hugs,
and time folds back and back
into your giant bearhug.
I am child again.

Any sea-smell / water-fragrance / sun-sparkle /
splash of harbor-water against a boat bottom
and there you are,
ocean-drunk,
in sneakers and captain's hat.

A benevolent host -
more than fifty years a ghost -
you preside over ritual festivities.
Unaware, I raise a glass,
and you are there!

THE BLUE SPRUCE CAFE

My father woke from his thirty-year sleep
and spoke to me
in the nowhere of vast northern woods.
The waitress poured coffee and left to get our breakfast.
Sunlight brightened the blue tablecloth;
tree shadows fluttered a lacy overlay.

A slender thread of music insisted;
the unsung words in my father's voice:
   -When I grow too old to dream,
    I'll have you to remember.*

  I am twelve again, perched on the bench beside him.
  His long fingers easily reaching octaves,
  he coaxed romantic old songs out of the same piano
  that wouldn't sing for my fingers.
  He rolled his eyes,
   flirting with his entranced little girl.
    -Sweet summer breeze,
     whispering trees,...
     kiss me, kiss me again.+

The pancakes absorbed syrup like rain on sand.
   -When I grow too old to dream
    that kiss will live in my heart.*
The music drifted to silence.
My father went back to sleep.

WHEN I GROW TOO OLD TO DREAM:
Words by Oscar Hammerstein; Music by Sigmund Romberg
+*KISS ME AGAIN*:
Words by Harry Blossom; Music by Victor Herbert

FLAT TIRE, FLUSHING, L.I. (CIRCA 1909)

    She picked a hazelnut from the dish
    as I set glasses of wine on the table.
    Our moments softened, and
    Mom surprised me with a nearly forgotten tale.

As a little girl, she skipped along the sidewalk,
her dress swinging around her knees.
She stopped, one foot
poised on the bottom porch step.
    Who was the beautiful lady in the feathered hat
    rocking on her mama's porch?
She eased up one step
as Mama elbowed through the screen door
with a tray of glasses and lemonade.

At the edge of the road, her papa
and a man in chauffeur's uniform struggled
to change a tire on the biggest car she'd ever seen!
The little girl inched closer to the car,
heard the chauffeur promise to return Papa's tire tomorrow
after he fixed the damaged one.

-Come, dear, I want you to meet Miss Sarah Bernhardt.
She's waiting in the shade while they fix her car.
    Miss Bernhardt smelled so nice!
    Big rings sparkled on her fingers.
She must have rocked in the shade for half an hour.
Then she thanked Mama for her kindness and rode away
in the big black car.
    Papa never saw his tire again!

    We sipped our wine.
    Mom was past ninety and I over sixty.
    In all these years,
    what stories has she not told me?

1944

The summer passed in apprehension.
It isn't often that
we see transitions coming.

    -You'll need extra underwear and towels.
    -Too bad we can't meet your roommate, choose bedspreads.
    -No! Don't take your radio!
        Suppose she has one too!

Dad circled 'round and around to find a place to unload the car
and muddled into confusion:
    joyous greetings,
    struggling fathers,
    admonishing mothers,
    seniors directing like sergeants.

The room - an appalling mess -
was smaller for two than my room at home.
    My roommate had claimed her bed,
    dumped her junk, and dashed away.
My mother, wanting to make the bed,
    rummaged and fussed
    ignoring my protests.

She burst into the room...
    -You're here!
    -My name's Faith, but call me Stinky.
    -Last year they called me Filth.
        ...and disappeared in a blur of flame-red hair.

And so began
        the lessons in coping,
        the dissolving of innocence.

BABS - 1947

Blonde - more than blonde!
She sauntered with shoulders pressed back,
a ball of yarn thrust into her blouse,
and carried about three inches of knitting on needles,
books under her arm.
Never saw her knit!

She smiled and smiled.
The boys' eyes rolled along after her.

He asked me to the prom months ago.
She led him around like a happy pup.
I watched, hurting,
needing to know which of us would go to the dance.
Should I even want to go?

At last he said he wanted to go with me,
sorry for my pain.

A month later, she was expelled -
something about a visit to the boys' dorm.

She took her knitting with her.

WHAT I WISH I'D KNOWN ABOUT THE PROM

Accept a date with the first – maybe only – guy
who calls.
It is the polite thing to do.

Choose a dress to scandalize your Dad and
make your Mom jealous...black or red velvet,
silver or gold lame, strapless.
You'll be ready to take on the girls, friends
and otherwise!
And the guys will stare.

He'll come in, late,
his pom-pom chick flirting her cute little butt.
Your date will have to share you with all of them,
all lined up for their turn on the dance floor.
You know how to dance, head up,
shoulders back,
legs and hips knowing all the moves.

Don't give him first dibs.
Make him wait his turn. Be cool
as your red velvet heats him up.
Move on and don't look back.

He'll be on the phone tomorrow!

MOVING - APRIL 1965

One by one,
everything we owned –
chairs, three beds and a crib,
two-and-a-half rugs, the kitchen table –
all, everything

was swallowed by the empty maw
of the moving van.
At last the vast doors rolled shut,
the truck less than half full.

We swept the floor,
locked the door,
and followed.

How long we had waited ...
and now watched from the foyer
as the van started half a block down,
gunned the engine,
plowed through the mud in the yard,
and sank to the hubcaps inches from the front step.

All, everything
scattered meagerly around the new house:
beds, two dressers, sofa,
table in the kitchen, nothing in the dining room,
books in boxes in the library.

As we turned to the daunting beginnings
in our new home,
two men struggled to liberate the truck,
inching, creeping back to the road,
spinning a rain of muck.

MUSEUM ART CLASS

-I made a candleholder for you, Mom.

Inside the package, a winged dinosaur,
    claws holding
      a birthday candle.

BEACH WONDERS

The children stride the beach,
heads bent searching for beach wonders.

Look! Look!
and they display a horseshoe crab
as though in their discovery they had created it.
A tentative toe turns it over -
exclamations of wonder -
and they move away to search further.

Pockets and shoes and hands filled with treasure,
they kneel in a mystic circle to count their hoard,
a ritual eons old.

They perform their rite and -
pleased with adventure -
gather up their wonders not knowing
that there is no marvel offered by the beach and sea
more marvelous than they.

THE RITUAL

-Your parents are here!
and there they are: Mom and Dad, and Grandma
and brother and sisters.

-Mom, Grandma, these are my friends, Ron and Jane.
-No, no, they were just leaving anyway.
All squeeze into the small room and find places to sit,
then agree as one to go on to the restaurant.

They are pleased,   -Your room is so neat!
a little wistful,   -We don't see you much anymore.
a trifle awed,   -Your studies are so complicated.
They see maturity blooming in their child.

Yet they seem so unchanged, so static,
compared with the vitality of ideas vibrating in college.

I have felt this distance
spreading between my parents and me
as I stand at the vital center.

Only now, I am outside the center.
      It has repeated.
      I am the parent.

DAUGHTER / DAUGHTER

You would have pulled out my tongue and -
with blank eyes-
bitten it into small pieces,
watched my words fall.

You would not hear,
nor would you speak.

We circled each other in small space
like wrestlers sizing up each other's
weakness.

My tongue has healed.
Now, I'm proud of you
and watch your daughter collect your golden words,
entranced, believing,
as you once were.

Even so, her circles widen.
At less than two, she tosses her head,
refuses to look at you, her mouth stitched shut.

Can you stay inside her circle,
hold the focus of her eyes,
and never watch together

as your tongue shatters into silent shards?

QUIET ROOMS

It's so nice that these rooms are always neat...
    no piles of clothes scattered 'round the floors,
    the spreads iced smoothly on the beds,
    and books, vertical, in rows upon the shelves.

These rooms are always neat...
    no music drifts down the hall,
    no lights burn at night;
    their life-spirit has gone,
    lives now in other homes, at school, away.

The vitality shall return, briefly,
    to churn and disarray the neatness of these rooms
    and throb with light and music,

but, too soon, to depart for ever-longer lengths of time
    until they shall be always
    neat and quiet.

BRET ANDREW, FEBRUARY 5, 2003

I smiled all day:
this is the kind of news
that can set the tilting world
up straight.

A new person arrived,
eyes squeezed against the glare,
fists holding tight
the dreams of his prenatal sleep.

He is all possibility, watching
his narrow world with wide dark eyes,
searching for meaning
in sound and speech.

He has no opinions,
has yet to learn the stories, to taste
bread and onions, to flex muscles
in a great leap, or share ideas.

He knows nothing of how land folds
as it swells into mountains,
of garden fragrance coaxed onto night air
by the silver invitation of the moon.

I smiled all day,
rocking with the tilting world.

PREPARING THE HOLE

I plant a Today rose,
white as the future.
I scoop and scrape, digging
to create its place in the earth.

With every dip into the hole,
I remove skeins and balls of yarn,
sweaters knitted by my mother.
Florence's embroidered pillowcases rise
with fragrance of Howard's farmyard spiraling
upward, entwined
with spray from waves splashing the hull
of my father's boat.

Even deeper, I find
Lucy's lemon pie and crocheted lace,
Auntie's beads and bangles,
Gramp's fishing pole, Papa's carpentry tools,
Evelyn's veiled hat and white gloves.

Today I plant the rose,
white as tomorrow,
creating
my place on earth.

THE WINDING TRAIL OF EXPLORERS' DREAMS

UNWINDING

The engine drones.
Scenery unwinds from the future
and pours past the windows like rain.

Needs recede,
drift into the past.

Unknown cities star the possibilities,
strung on ribbons of rivers,
tucked into folds of mountains.

An uncluttered room waits.
Life simplifies.
Sleep.

Tomorrow
      -a museum of marvels
      -a mountain waiting to be touched
      -an ocean searching the beach for wanderers
      -time unwinding slowly,
           easing away unnoticed on a scented wind.

ART EXHIBIT

We strolled the edges of the lily pond at Giverny,
stared transfixed at sun-drenched haystacks,
and floated along a misty river beside light-veiled poplars.

Drawn into diffused light and pastel shadow,
we moved through the green and flowers
of the untidy garden,
crossed the Chinese bridge.

A mauve cathedral shimmered by sunset glow,
steam haloed engines in the glass-roofed station ...
we could hear the humming, the hissing.

Driving home,
we crossed a bridge over a wooded ravine,
reflection and shadow dancing,
mist rising from the rocky stream.

Our little girl cried in delight,
      -Oh, what Monet could do with that!

WASHINGTON METRO

Within the windows of the subway car,
a train runs parallel

carrying identical passengers,
who are staring, reading, nodding.

In that alternative world, a woman in a short skirt
leans against the balance pole, swaying,

a man with hairy arms bends forward in his seat
and shrugs into his jacket,

a small boy with penny-bright hair squirms beside his mother,
her coppery mane a vivid shawl on her shoulders,

a skinny man with a scruffy beard
nods above an open briefcase.

The train ticks its monotonous rhythm,
the phantom car silent, people swaying.

Tenleytown ... both trains stop;
identical doors hush open. Passengers crowd through,

blend with their shadow-selves
and move across the platform toward the stairs.

CHICAGO IN SUMMER

1
He lies on the stone bench,
back to the concrete embankment above the river.
People pass.
Traffic flows in surges and pauses -
yellow cabs, a bicycle.
Heat vibrates from the glass towers.
His red shirt proclaims,
"I am!"

2
The warning bell begins. The walkway gate snaps shut.
Traffic piles up.
Pedestrians, leaning over the wide wall,
watch seven sailboats circling in the river below,
two lashed together.
A bongo drummer pounds a relentless beat,
countering the steadfast bell.

The roadbed lifts - a giant cage, slanting upward.
Single file, the boats glide through.
The bongos build a crescendo!
The bell chimes as the roadbed lowers.
Traffic roars through;
people stream across the bridge.
The drummer's trapped audience vanishes.

3
Thunder rumbles down the city canyons.
Lightning flickers,
haloes concrete towers,
stabs down the narrow fissures.
Rain beats on glass, on garbage cans,
on cars splashing in the murky light.
People hunch under umbrellas.
The golden glow from stacked windows offers
no refuge.
Thunder snarls.

CITY SUMMER NIGHT

The city calms in the night,
    cools in the night,
    but hums a low moan.

A car glides past in a hush of air -
    then a sudden call, a thrill of laughter,
    and quick silence.

The hum resumes
    and shatters into a scream of sirens.
    The city-song never ceases.

The hum dissolves as a truck labors, shifting gears.
    It rumbles to a stop, groans around the corner,
    and fades into the endless hum.

A car door slams, brief voices and footsteps echo
    as the hum changes volume in the distance
    and subsides.

Another swish of a passing car...
    and the city sings its night song,
    droning low its relentless hum.

VICKSBURG

The traveler follows a sculptured parkway,
memorial to the death-rattle of the States which died aborning.
Woodlands and smooth hillsides conceal forever
the debris of battle.
Monuments repeat the tales of valor and defeat,
maps outline the rise and fall of strategy,
but nowhere on these grounds is recorded
the anguish of human loss,
the gut-wrenching fear.

Forty-seven days of not knowing...
but knowing well that the end had come.
Caring for the wounded,
a young wife yearned toward the gunfire,
every explosion in her stomach for her husband.
Housekeeping underground,
she soothed her hungry toddlers with meaningless promises.
Women, keening every hour for the young and strong
brought home for burial,
struggled to sustain sanity for the living.

Rows and rows of grave markers,
grinning skull-teeth in velvet grass,
haunt the traveler as he passes.

Remember us!
We were men who sired sons,
     sat at table laughing,
     wept at the wake of friend or brother,
     danced at village fairs,
     held life as dearly as you.
We put our faith on the line and died with our cause.
Pass our graves.
Visit our battleground.
     But remember us;
     remember!

GRAND CANYON

Sister Hawk,
your wings lean on waves of wind
as you glide and tilt
along strands of sun.

Take me into your fine feathers and sail down,
down steep folded walls,
red, purple, cream,
prickly with cactus and desert scrub.
Tiny flames of red and yellow bloom,
embroidered tightly into pleated rock.

Take me down the long sweep
of canyon crossing canyon crossing
ravine and gulch and arroyo,
down to the glossy ribbon of river,
where cottonwoods dig long toes
into tenuous damp.

I spread my wings with yours, Sister Hawk,
in our long slow glide between narrow red walls,
rapids foaming below,
waters chanting a song of eons,
of eras of rock and upheaval,
of seas and sands,
forests, thriving and falling.

Lifting upward,
we escalate through layers of earth-history,
the river receding,
wind vibrating beneath us.

Farewell, Sister Hawk!
My feet back on the top layer of Time,
I walk my steady step in
Now.

HIGHWAY CALIFORNIA

The landscape rises
and folds into mountains and ravines.

A road of many esses follows the winding trail
of explorer's dreams

between slopes of parched grasses,
through dark tunnels of evergreen.

Hawks glide in a searing sky above cattle
huddled on the floor of an arid creek.

Trees stretch higher, close in,
and filter sunlight into golden pools among the ferns.

"Yorkville, population 25."
Silvered buildings stare into the empty street.

A skeleton of old fence staggers
over the crest of a hill,

stops at the brink of a cliff
where ocean spray reaches up with white fingers.

DENALI / MCKINLEY

We spent three days with the mountain.
The natives told us
that she did not reveal herself to everyone.
She pulls the mists around her shoulders
and retires into imperious seclusion.

Approaching by train,
snowy peaks snugging the valley,
we wound along rivers,
through rocky plains and forests, colored
russet and gold.

We glimpsed her diamond tiara,
her ermine cloak of clouds,
always as if she were floating above the earth.

A long bus ride delivered us closer to her feet,
yet she remained remote.
In the cold air sweeping down from glaciered slopes,
we sipped hot drinks
and pondered her inscrutability.

We departed by train,
fireweed flaming beside the tracks,
the mountain keeping pace with our racing wheels,
distant,
a vaporous dream.

PYRAMIDS OF TEOTIHUACAN

In light clothing yet wilting
under a dazzling blue sky –
a sky you wouldn't believe in a painting –
we dodge a gauntlet of vendors.

> Ragged, dark-eyed children cry, Holà! Holà!
> and block our way with trays of trinkets.
> Adults offer "real silver"
> and pottery copies of Aztec treasure.

We edge around them
and enter a civilization
that could have descended from a far-away galaxy:
a culture of geometry and architecture.

> The pyramids tower over barren land,
> depict on chamber walls the faces
> of the vendors we passed,
> harvests of grain, priests in feathered robes.

Drawn by ancient mysteries,
we explore high narrow rooms and columned corridors,
sacrificial platforms.
History flows on a pathway of golden heat.

> The bus is leaving.
> We drive through the centuries
> on the dusty road.

OAXACANA

Raw sunlight slashes down the wall,
casts barred shadows on the walk.

Near the corner,
a small brown woman,
centuries old,
curls against the crumbling wall
in shade sculpted by brutal light,
legs folded under her skirt, where
passersby step around, ignoring
her pleading hand.

Two children sprawl
against her shoulder,
across her lap.
They do not move,
do not speak,
do not cry.

CATHEDRAL CONCERT, OAXACA

A pigeon sleeps on God's shoulder
at the top of the pyramid of saints, holding
birds in the crooks of their elbows.
Night hawks swoop around the bell tower
in a blaze of lights.

Families gather in the plaza,
fill the rows of chairs.
Lovers hold each other on the stone wall;
a little girl lets her balloon sail off into the night.
A man hands us his program, nods
to our smiles and "Gracias!"

Strains of Beethoven soothe the audience to silence.
Rhythms of a polka dance away
under the poincianas edging the plaza.
Silver notes of a trumpet blow on the night wind
into stars shimmering
above God's shoulder.

FRANCE - AFTER ALL THESE YEARS

The massive ship rises on an air cushion
glides, roaring, from Dover to Calais.
Passengers descend to the cluttered tarmac,
cluster to collect baggage and relatives,
gradually disappear.

> *Je suis ici... Je suis arrivée...*
> *Après tous les ans que je l'ai voulu,*
> *Je suis arrivée!*

My feet stand rooted where Henry V landed with his men
on their way to victory at Agincourt
and returned with Catherine, his prize, his queen.
Anne Boleyn, only seven, jumped ashore at Calais
following her sister to the court of François,
where she absorbed fashion and intrigue
and set her course toward tragedy.
Centuries later, a tidal wave of young men
poured onto the beach into a rain of death.

History surges beneath my feet,
tilts the ripened fields of Van Gogh.
Had Jeanne heard her voices whispering
in wind riffling the grain?
Is that the woodland road,
silvered by Debussy's moonlight,
where Dumas sent his musketeers
on their desperate ride to save a kingdom?

> I am here ... I have arrived ...
> After all the years that I have wished it ...
> *Je suis arrivée!*

THE STREETS OF ROUEN

Maman and two little girls in cotton dresses
trudge up the cobbled street, wary
of cars behind in the narrow road.
Grey stone buildings, windows shuttered,
crowd the uneven walk.

Maman and big sister climb the steep, uneven road,
each with a package from their trip to the market.
Little sister follows, carrying
a baguette in a paper sleeve,
the long bread almost as tall as she.

>   As she toils up the rough road, lagging
>   behind maman and sister,
>   she licks the brown crust bobbing under her chin.

THE BELLS OF NURNBURG

Deep tones roll down the cobbled slope
away from the stone cathedral,
splash up the shop walls in waves,
reverberate underfoot.

Worshippers climb the uneven road
engulfed in iron murmur,
bronze thunder
intoning an invitation to praise their Lord.
Little girls in white dresses carry flowers
and baskets of fruit.

Swinging, surging, cascading -
echoes tumble into the morning,
torrents of tenor – baritone – bass.
The bells soothe and disturb,
purr and mourn.
The heaviest tone slows, tolls... tolls...
dissolves
into Sunday silence.

GOURNIA, CRETE

Ariadne, Phaedra, Daphne –
I invade your hospitality without invitation,
wander in your atrium,
in the great room where you served honeyed wine
to your husbands' guests.
I hear your children's calls
where they ran on the hillsides with the sheep and goats.

Phaedra, your pestle grates on the wind
where you ground grain for bread.
The scent of leather rises in the heat, cured
by Daphne to craft sandals for her sons.
Your spinning wheel, Ariadne, whispers
in the corner where you spun wool for fine robes.

Smoke from your lamps rises with mist
into the mountains.

Ariadne, Phaedra, Daphne –
are you watching by your doorways
as I pace your floors,
intrude upon your hospitality?
Could we have sat together at the same loom
weaving for the queen
a pattern in lapis and gold,
laughing and gossiping,
sisters in another millennium?

VENICE IN OCTOBER

Rain silvers the cobbles,
floats bubbles under moored gondolas.
Like colorful mushrooms, umbrellas bloom on walks,
bob over staired bridges

Undaunted, pigeons waddle, swarming
among the tourists.
Undaunted, tourists wander, swarming
among the shops.

Sunlight glimmers ...
song rises in the water canyons.
A gondola glides by,
oarsman balanced on the rear deck.
Accordionist and tenor serenade along the water corridors,
bow to applause from walks and bridges.

A waterbus spills passengers,
opens its wide mouth to swallow more ...
    -students with black, purple, red backpacks
    -a woman with wine-red hair
    -business men with briefcases and running shoes
They ebb and flow with the rolling waves,
step off the rocking dock
onto a rocking deck.

In a spate of rain,
tourists shoulder into boutiques offering
amazements of glass ...
a vast museum of the exquisite,
the extravagant, the extraordinary.

Showers subside
and evening soothes the plaza;
patrons savor espresso at outdoor cafes,
drink in the liquid melodies of waltz and opera
poured from accordion, violin, piano.
Passersby pause, listen, applaud,
then stroll on to the next café.

Wet cobbles gleam under the glow
from the great cathedral,
dozing pigeons murmur among the friezes,
waves splash the hulls of moored boats.

WHITE NIGHT, FINLAND

In evening glow an hour before midnight,
    the lake shimmers turquoise and crimson,
    lapping, murmuring.

On a boulder, a tiny island fifty ripples from the dock,
    a seagull settles in her nest,
    one eye watchful.

A silver disc ascends the eastern sky;
    the sun smears red
    on clouds swimming in still water.

Towering pines
    shadow the shore,
    the only dark.

Hours later and wakeful
    in other-worldly light,
    I stand at the window.

The lake gleams under white sky,
    the high moon snagged
    in the top of a pine.

    Twilight
        white night
            dawnlight

GUILIN, CHINA

Mountains rise from the valley floor like dragons
drinking clouds,
their tails swirling in fog.

The silver river flows out of the mist;
fishing skiffs nuzzle the shore,
waiting.

Water buffalo graze in the rice fields
behind tile-roofed cottages.
Three women kneel

on a stone landing,
wringing water from their laundry.
The serene river shimmers in sunlight.

The mountains pierce clouds
like heads
of giant dragons.

ANCIENT CITY, SUZHOU

A purple tree-of-many-fragrances
bends toward the water; orange sun
spills into the canal and crinkles.

A barge chugs, rumbles,
freighted to the gunwales,
passes the watergate

and under the staired bridge, arched
high over the canal.
Laundry spins on lines hung

along the walk.
A bright mosaic of teapots, toys
and scarves

patterns tables outside the shops,
and bikes flow down the streets,
part of the great rivers...

relentless rivers of people,
rivers of traffic,
rivers of boats,

rivers of water
flowing through China,
flowing.

RAINBOWS FROM MY PRISMS

MY FRIEND / MY LOVER / MY CHILD

Smile and greet me warmly when we meet;
we've been apart for long and long a day
and ever has our parting tasted bittersweet.

Once our dance together kept a measured beat
before you bowed and turned to step away.
Smile and greet me warmly when we meet.

I wait and weep, remembering the sweet
and poignant past before the day
since ever has our parting tasted bittersweet.

You must test the wings upon your feet -
flying, falling, seeking out your way.
Smile and greet me warmly when we meet

then go again; explore a stranger street
and never really hear me say
that ever has our parting tasted bittersweet.

Freedom shall be yours, my love, my sweet;
love is not love that bars the way.
Smile and greet me warmly when we meet
for ever has our parting tasted bittersweet.

FRIENDSHIP
Patricia McNair: December 1927 – October 2007

"We play hooky better than any people I know!"
She smiled at my comment,

and off we went
to see an art exhibit because it was the last day.
We would call three friends
to go walking in the autumn woods
and then drive to a neighboring town
to find a restaurant someone recommended.
Three or five of us would meet for lunch
and share new poems, old poems, found poems,
and photographs of grandchildren
or our last outing together.

The young man at UPS put the counter
in the copy machine before we opened the door
and then stood by to be sure "back-to-back"
was inserted correctly.

We were insatiable for books –
any excuse to visit Barnes & Noble ...
to find a birthday gift for a grandchild,
to browse in a new collection by Mary Oliver,
to see if the recent Harry Potter has been
translated into Spanish ...
and we often left sharing a bargain treasure
we couldn't resist.

One bitter late autumn evening,
we covered the flowers in her garden
to save them for a few more precious days.

We never ran out of conversation
and were never bored by silence –
we could just be.

A LOVE POEM

Without him, the sun would shine
but not for me
who would wonder why the brightened sky!

Could I stride the crest of glittering snow
and gulp the brittle air
without his trail ahead among the winter trees?
Could I crush summer fragrance from a forest floor
without his footsteps keeping pace with mine?
A soothing rhythm, a tempo of two,
flows through our winters and bright summers.

We've exulted as one
as wondrous music filled our senses,
but could I bear to hear
were he not there?
The works of master artists would be as rare
but not for me
without him to share!

Our fingers stroke to warm
or strike sparks of fire;
his smile smoothes silkenly through my soul.
I do love and would love others
in other ways,
       but, without him,
       sunshine would lure no rainbows from my prisms.

VOWS

We were asked, long ago, to honor, cherish, and love -
and thus were promised,
    thought we loved,
        believed in honor and cherishing.
            It was early and we were young.

We have walked long down the corridor of time
and know now that there is depth and dimension in love
    unplumbed by those whose flames burn high and bright.
    The flame spreads and deepens,
        firing and molding.

We have faceted our marriage
and are polishing with the abrasions of living.
    We have refined patience,
        have become more individual and more
            together as the path lengthens behind us.

We have learned to honor and cherish and love
and shall learn.

THE WEDDING POEM
Composed for the wedding of
Bonnie Presson and Mark Tincknell, August 22, 1981

Love each other with laughter,
and you shall love each other also with your tears.
Share your joy,
and your sharing shall deepen in disappointment.

You receive freedom from your gift of trust,
and your consideration one for the other will give you peace.
Grant your courtesy to each other as to your dearest friend,
for dear friends you must be to be dear lovers.

Temper your irritation with understanding
so that your love may fuse into enduring strength.
As you encourage each other's dreams,
your own dreams will be nourished.

Let patience weave itself among your enthusiasms
that time may reveal their importance in the patterns of your life;
and live in the shelter of God's love
that He may sustain you in your need.

Finally, in the silence of your years,
you will discover that your love and your dreams,
your laughter and your tears
have accomplished your marriage.

LITTLE BRACELETS OF FLAME
This is a little bracelet of flame around your wrist
— Charles Wright

We descend the steps of a bus
        and fall into step together, following
a guide through ruins of a civilization
three millennia past.
        Our hands brush and clasp.

We spin through revolving doors
        and fall into step together, following
the busy, noisy streets of a civilization
rushing into the future.
        Our hands brush and clasp.

We step on a fragrant carpet under trees
        and fall into step together, following
a path of non-civilization
from before the past to beyond the future.
        Our hands brush and clasp ...
        sending up little bracelets of flame.

LOVE SEASONS

I spring-love you ...
    -a pastel, new-growth,
    blooming-into-discovery love.

I summer-love you ...
    -a hot-sand, water-silk,
    forest-shadow, thunder-and-rain love.

I autumn-love you ...
    -a color-flurry, crunchy-leaves,
    apple-juicy, spin-in-the-wind love.

I winter-love you ...
    -a wood-smoke, candlelight,
    quilt-cozy, warm-by-the-fire love.

THE GOLDEN CIRCLE

A tiny gold circle ...
part of my life
for more than fifty years.

We dated five months
when he left for home,
eight hundred miles away.

After months of letters, he returned
with his grandmother's ring – a gold circlet
entwined with grapes and leaves.

Next year,
the same date in June,
we married, exchanging gold rings.

Our golden years
hold us
in our golden circle.

COMFORT

1
The baby leaned
away from me
toward her.

I said,
There is no comfort
 like a mother's arms.

She smiled,
then, holding her son,
moved into my arms.

2
A rightness with the world
comes in with him
when he opens the door.

The house feels complete,
that bit of emptiness
filled.

As the door closes,
we are
contained.

Wine poured, we sit
silent, conversing,
comfortable.

THE TOY SHOP

He unpacked the toys, helping her,
    soft-bodied animals,
        dolls with silky hair.

Croquet balls spilled, rolling away.
    She reached,
        gathering them into a narrow box.

His eyes filled with her
    as she leaned away.
        Her hand brushed his thigh.

They built a pyramid of blocks.
    He inflated balloons;
        the smooth skin clung to his lip.

She turned the key on a music box
    and a light melody lifted
        into the room.

They moved with the toys,
    placing them...
        plush bears in their hands,

balls filling boxes,
    towers of blocks, building
        higher...   higher.

RENDEZVOUS

He mounted the stairs ... slowly,
sliding his hand along the banister
as it curved upward.
Sunlight blazed through the window on the landing
where the stairs turned
and led him on into the upper corridor.

The door opened
and he entered.

Framed against the glow of an oval mirror,
she placed a rosebud
into a tapered vase
and apricots in a porcelain saucer.
Her fingers traced the fringes of a blond shawl
shimmering in folds upon the table.

They sat opposite each other,
the fruit between them.
He drank from the cup she offered
as, slowly,
she peeled the smooth skin,
dropped it
empty
upon the plate.

JUST DESSERT

He waited,
sipped the hot drink.

She set the sweets before him,
    sat down,
        her foot touching his.

A taper glowed,
    flame at the tip;
    a melody licked into their ears.

They dipped into the thick dessert,
    savored the satin and cinnamon,
    cream slicking their tongues.

Their spoons moved along the curve of the dish,
    penetrated to the center,
    lifted sweets into their mouths.

They lingered
    over flavors, fragrances;
    emptied the bowl.

Music drifted into shadow;
the flame flickered.

GODIVA'S SECRET

When does a woman initiate her daughter,
reveal to her that dark pleasure,
open her to indulgence, the black sweet bitterness,
the reliable solace.

If she is quite young,
she might start her with a silver kiss,
a beginning.

Soon, though, they share it hot, steaming
in a cold winter twilight,
savoring fragrance, flavor, texture.
The seduction escalates,
and each understands that the other will arrange
her own assignations.

At times, they will indulge, purely,
voluptuously - and alone.
There will be meetings with others, laughing,
and pretense that the extravagance is rare.
But then, the need...
when the weave of existence tangles,
when the volcano of confusion rumbles,
when the sheets on the bed turn cold.

Woman to woman, they share the dark secret.

SECRETS THEY DO NOT SHARE

"ALL THE MONKEYS AREN'T IN THE ZOO"
From "Swinging on a Star" with music composed by Jimmy Van Heusen and lyrics by Johnny Burke.

Wallabies, leopards and tigers and bears
are patiently living at home in the zoo
enduring a crowd of curious stares.

Winters and summers without any cares,
they sit in a cage and gaze back at you,
wallabies, leopards and tigers and bears.

If you were dining or climbing your stairs,
how would you feel and what would you do,
enduring a crowd of curious stares?

Could you happily dance alone or in pairs
even if watched by only a few
wallabies, leopards and tigers and bears?

Would you change your clothes and put on airs
if you found yourself, like the cockatoo,
enduring a crowd of curious stares?

Now, when you go to examine their lairs,
think how the animals look upon you,
wallabies, leopards and tigers and bears,
enduring a crowd of curious stares!

LEOPARD

He lies stretched along a branch
high above the jungle floor,
dozing, watching,
his fur a camouflage of sunlight and shadow.

If anything moves,
he knows.
He is a camera, focusing images –
      the herd of zebras
      giraffes stilt-walking the horizon
      elands with a weak elder limping in their wake.

A monkey chatters above,
keeping his distance.
The leopard watches,
waits.

NICHOLAS

He tours his domain, scenting
the prowlers of the night,
deposits his conquests by the terrace door,
meditates on his shaded fence post.

As the car rumbles into the garage, he emerges
from his cool cave beneath the evergreens
to meet us halfway in the drive,
tail rising in a flag of welcome.

In the cool of moonlit nights,
he sits atop the chimney, counting stars.
Summer afternoons, he lounges on the roof,
a diminutive gargoyle leaning over the eaves
to spy on those who pass below.

His eloquent silence lets us know
we are his,
lets us know – his back turned –
that it is time to present his supper.

In the night,
absolutely certain of his rights,
he curls on the bed between our feet,
purring.

PUSSY CAT, PUSSY CAT, WHERE HAVE YOU BEEN?

At night my kitty loves to prowl,
is ever too polite to howl!
But, just as I drift off to sleep,
outside my window kitty creeps
and, crying there, he pats and scratches,
steals my sleep away in snatches
until I open up the door
and, finally, return to snore.

Then on my bed, he turns around,
cozily he settles down
exactly where I place my feet
and, peacefully, he falls asleep.
I'm finally about to dream
with kitty curled, asleep it seems,
when a secret whisper in his ear
sets him marching, tail like a spear,
up and down my tired self,
a furry, mischievous, four-legged elf.

Resigned, I plunk my feet to the floor,
go back again to open the door!

HAYLEY IN MIDDLE AGE

She bursts out of the van,
dances circles in fallen oak leaves,
and dashes along the old road dividing the woods.
She tastes a puddle in mid-path,
then spirals from tree to bush
nosing out the local news.
Down a slope and back up,
she pauses with a quizzical look,
wondering why two-legged folk are so slow.

The late sun switches on light behind golden maples
and sends a glittering path across the lake
where she plunges in,
swims a circle,
and emerges grinning and shaking stars
into the bright afternoon.
Another dive for a stick and shower of stars ...
then wrestling, growling, chewing,
and a luxurious roll on a bed of leaves.

A little slower at last,
she tastes another puddle,
trots on toward the van
and a nap.

MIGRATION NORTH

Their raucous squawking, like flying dogs,
lifts my thin gauze of sleep
as they flap in the moonless dark
               to their marshy flats.

Neighborhood dogs, tethered to earth,
send their meager cries to the freedom skies.

Through sheer draperies of my dream,
I fly with them on wings of rain.
The geese and I fly north,
               writing our poems on the wind.

SEA GULL

He jerks along the wooden rail on prong-foot stilts,
surveys the silken ocean
which thunders with the sound of cloth unrolled
and snapped hard
and hard again.
A statue, he stares above the panorama below.

Couples stride along the tide line,
children build their dreams in sand,
sun worshippers sprawl in their baptism of heat,
and young men plunge through breakers,
ride them up and down,
waiting,
waiting for the perfect crest
to take them on a fast slide to the shallows,
where they rise and plunge again.

Not a flicker of his red eye as he stands in the white light.

The beach will be deserted at nightfall.
He will be alone
to scavenge their debris
and soar above the moving sea in the fading twilight.

SEAGULL SYMPHONY

Seven seagulls – no, nine –
perch on the roof-rim of the band shell,
beaks pointed to the azure sky.
A flutter of wings, a ruffle of tail feathers,
and three gulls turn to face the other way
as music rises in a crescendo of horns and drums.

Flutes shrill, the marimba dances,
a soprano sings of mountains and golden wheat.
More birds swoop in to listen,
stepping carefully in small circles.

When the audience applauds,
all fifteen leap into the air.

The music resumes, and
they gradually return to their grandstand on the roof,
bathed in waves of sound
and golden light of the setting sun.

Do seagulls attend concerts in the park
because they cannot sing?

PIGEONS

They waddle on the walk
like dumpy ladies dressed for Sunday.
They strut and stop,
nodding, murmuring.

Their colors muted –
pale grey,
beige, caped in rust,
and black with white skirt –

every one jeweled in emerald and amethyst.
The ladies bustle about their invisible errands,
cluster to exchange their gossip,
then separate to shop beneath the azaleas.

MALLARD

No sooner had I sat on the weathered bench
than he flicked his tail to steer his tiny ship
and waddled up the gentle slope,
pecking at the wet grass
as if he really hadn't come expecting crumbs from me.

He circled three times and zigzagged
until he re-entered his rippled-silk pond.

With a nod of his green-velvet head,
he joined the flotilla of golden leaves
and sailed across the melted fires of autumn,
chuckling as though he knew a secret he had not shared.

THE MAGICAL SHIMMER

THE QUEEN REFLECTS
- twenty years after she married the beast-prince -

What can she see in him?
When she brought him home to meet me, he growled,
    -Hey, lady, what's happ'nin'? toothpick hanging
        from his teeth and reeking of beer and cigarettes.

They roared under the porte cochère on his motorcycle
and spun to a stop, spraying the footman and foyer with dirt.
    No apology. He grabbed her under the arms,
        whirled her off the seat, kissed her in front of the servants.

My daughter, attracted to that! She attended the finest schools,
studied history, French, art, and violin.
    Now she wears batik robes, leather and beads in her hair.
    Walks with her hand in his back pocket.

He dropped out of everything.
Runs with a crowd of bikers,
        racing in mud and sand.
        Hair like a raveled sweater!

Then she throws her father up to me!
Her father was as different ... well, there's no comparison!
    We did not begin well, it's true, but,
        by the time of the witch-change, I loved him.

I hadn't expected a handsome prince in my bridal bed,
but his renaissance brought an onslaught of women!
    Even my sisters fluttered
    like moths to the light!

Well, perhaps <u>she</u> will not know the anguish of jealousy!
She will stay with her lover whether I approve or not
        and possibly be happier because
        a witch-change will not "improve" her prospects!

THE SLEEPING BEAUTY

It was a daddy's dream that,
on the brink of her dance into her future,
his little girl should sink into oblivion
and sleep for a hundred years,
secure behind stone walls and bramble bushes.

He could relax his vigil and sleep too.

Inevitably,
the awakening would come.
Drawn by her mystic innocence,
an adventurer hacked his way through the brambles
and shoved the gate off its rusted hinges.

The young sojourner led her away from her overgrown bower.

By the time daddy awoke to his daughter's song,
he had to concede that a hundred years was as much
as a father could hope for.
He might as well have a party
to conceal his pain.

Did he care that she was riding into her sunrise
    -with a husband ninety-eight years younger than she?
    -that her trousseau was all vintage clothing
    destined for a stable sale?
    -that her minstrels would sing songs
    she wouldn't understand?

GLASS SHOES

They were the prettiest shoes
I ever saw!
They glittered in the firelight,
and I couldn't wait to try them on.

But I hadn't moved three steps down the elegant staircase
when I knew they were trouble.
Neither Godmother nor I had given a single thought
to how glass shoes would feel.
They don't bend!
How do you walk gracefully down a curved marble stair
when your shoes are as slippery as ice
and sound like someone knocking the towers off the castle?

But the Prince stood transfixed with a lopsided smile,
ignoring three princesses vying for his attention.
Stepping as lightly as possible,
I almost snatched his hand to keep my balance
on the bottom step and, leaning on his arm,
<u>slid</u> my feet toward the dance floor.
What next?
If he stepped on my toe,
would my shoe shatter?
If I turned too fast, would a heel snap off?
My toes felt as if they were broken.
Would anyone notice if I danced barefoot?

When that blessed clock struck twelve,
I raced for the palace gates,
grateful to limp home
to a basin of warm Epsom salts.

I didn't say a word when the whole countryside
was a-buzz over the lost slipper.
They could put it in a museum for all I care!

I didn't intend to try it on when the king's messenger
came to our house and my foolish sisters
kept trying to cram in their size-12 double-wides.
When I brought in goose grease for their feet,
he noticed me and insisted
that <u>every</u> young woman in the kingdom
had to be fitted.

I <u>was</u> glad to see the Prince again,
but now I have to wear sparkly glass shoes
every night to please him.
My only hope is that he won't want to dance!

THE LEGEND OF KYLA, HAWK WOMAN

>Long ago, in the time before time,
>Kyla walked among the northern trees,
>flew with Hawk on wings of Wind.

And animals moved in harmony with the sun and seasons.
Beaver built his home in the marshy streams;
Fox hunted along his secret trails.
Wolf and Bear sang and danced in their rhythms
of night and light.

>In the seasons of sun and rain,
>Kyla gathered the blue of distant mountains,
>the gold blaze of August meadows,
>the flame of September woodlands
>and wove them into long ribbons
>to cast into the rain-misted sky.

When Father Sun's children climb silver ladders of rain,
they hang Kyla's arc of colors between clouds and earth.

On a moonless night in Summer,
Hawk flew high in a turbulent sky and seized
a bolt of lightning from the talons of Thunderbird.

>Kyla twisted and molded and bent it to her will.
>She forged it into a fiery blade,
>axe and scythe and sword,
>which bit into the forest,
>felled the White Pine for her shelter.

>In Winter, Kyla built her hearth-fires,
>fanned them hot and hotter,
>melted the icecap over the Northern Pole.
>Icemelt flooded into Great Valley,
>became The Great Inland Sea.

In the swelter of Summer,
Bear and Wolf swam with Kyla in the Great Sea.
Rivulets overran the shores, filled vast valleys,
formed the Five Great Northern Seas.

    As Kyla arose in the glow of sunset,
    cascades of icy water foamed into Taquamenon,
    boiled over boulders,
    brewed a dark tea to feed the forest.

    She swung her midnight hair to dry,
    tossed glittering stars onto the Eastern dark.
    Flashes of green and blue flamed from her flying hair,
    fired the Northern Sky.

When Hawk soars into the rose-glow
low in the West,
and Wolf sends his Song to the rising Moon,
and the magical shimmer spreads long fingers up the charcoal sky,

    Kyla has stepped from her bath in Great Superior
    and stirs the Wind Spirits of Night
    as she swings her dark mantle of hair to dry.

THE LADY OF SHALOTT
–after a painting by James Perkins and Tennyson's Morte d'Arthur–

What do you prove, Lady,
setting yourself adrift to spite unrequited love?
He will go on,
your despair notwithstanding.
Launcelot, "most honorable knight,"
is an adulterer and murderer,
but your blood leaps at his beauty and panache.

When you turned to the window and the real world,
your mirror cracked. Now you drift,
unruddered, among reeds and water lilies,
tragedy in your eyes,
the chain connecting you to reality slipping
through your fingers.

Go back to your loom,
return to your artistry. Tell your story.
He is not worth your smallest tear
and will gallop off
with cavalier disregard of chaos behind him.

You drift on,
death in your heart for hopeless love.
Without remorse,
he will look on your white face and blank eyes,
and, as you will it,
offer a mass-penny for your funeral.

Would you journey on your blackened barge knowing
that he will spend the winter hawking and carousing
without reflection upon Elaine,
the Lily Maid of Astolat?

PUTTING ON BILLY COLLINS' CLOTHES
- after his poem, Taking Off Emily Dickinson's Clothes -

While he stares at watery reflections
in the dark windows and
dreams of setting sail around the room,
I tap his knee for attention and hold his briefs ...
left foot, right foot.
I slide the tee shirt over his ears -
right arm, left arm –
and smooth it around his waist.
Now the socks: brown socks, brown pants.
He sits as I gather them over his toes
and stretch them over his full calves.

He draws breath and sighs
as headlights cut a jagged swath across the ceiling
and he steps into the collapsed legs of his trousers;
I pull them up, snap the waist.
His head emerges slowly through the snug collar
of a beige turtleneck,
bobs slightly as I tug it into place on his shoulders
and twist the sleeves straight.
I open his waistband and tuck
all around, over belly and butt, snugging it down,
fastening snaps, zipping,
sliding his belt through the loops,
buckling the goldtone buckle.

Gathering the chocolate cable-knit sweater,
I ease it over the turtleneck,
arrange his sleeves and smooth the back.
As he steps into brown loafers,
I lift his left hand, turn back his cuff, and
encircle his wrist with his watch band.
Tugging slightly, I resettle his sleeves and
turn him to the mirror, brush his hair to the side,
and open the door.

SHADOW IN THE GLASS HOUSE
-in honor of the 100th anniversary of Theodore Roethke's birth, May 25, 2008-

A shadow flickers against the glass
like a passing cloud;
orchids exhale, breathing.
Dangling roots sway beneath roses
and geraniums in table trays
where a little boy creeps
until he hears his father's "Ordnung!"
and scrambles into the humid light.

Ghostly garden witches dance in the aisles,
conjuring dry seeds into bright flowers,
yanking weeds and dead blooms,
stringing stems and vines,
coaxing their pet from his cave,
laughing.

The boy-shadow moves against the sky,
arms reaching toward white clouds,
poems galloping eastward.

Chrysanthemums stare up at his wild ride.
"Ordnung!"
Papa's coming!

FREIGHT TRAIN

In the dark of morning,
the train three blocks away vibrates
through my room.
Its warning intersects my waking.

Pulling a jacket over pajamas,
I shove into shoes,
run across crackling brown grass,
and leap for the handle and step of a boxcar.
Holding on, holding on...
cold rushing air...
shaking....

The train clatters across empty streets,
passes behind garages in shadowed backyards,
parallels the silky river,
rattles over the iron bridge to East Saginaw,
crosses the deserted city.
It grumbles through the thinning night
into fields of corn stubble,
and groves of gaunt trees.

I fly with the train
into the rose-pearl of dawn,
sway with the rocking freight
into the possibilities
of distance.

BRASSY RHYTHM

Sound encircles my ears,
      surrounds my shoulders,
      spirals down around my feet,
      draws them, dancing, into a pool of light.

I dip – circle – slide,
      hips moving –
      head bobbing –
      arms undulating.

The music licks into my brain,
      fizzes in my hair.
      It is purple and crimson,
      flame and emerald,
      the thin, high fragrance of roses,
      pungency of cloves, and

drums pound chocolate,
      pound chocolate.

I glide on silver ice,
      roll with the ocean tides,
      moving,
      moving.

ALL THINGS CONSIDERED

TESTING THE OPTIONS

    All things considered,
    He was new at the creation business
    when He flung the Life Force from His open arms
    and guided it down the eons toward a tiny solar system
    in a distant galaxy.

He gradually got better at the details.
Those lumbering, mindless brutes were amusing for a few millennia,
but He finally got bored watching them eat up the landscape
every few centuries.
He seared them to cinders
and let the planet cool into a luscious paradise.
Tossed in some butterflies and songbirds and orchids.
Refining details.

    The setting was perfect for a life form
    that could savor the beauty.

He set Man and Woman on their feet
and let them play with His new toy.
He did not anticipate, however,
that they had nothing with which to compare their good fortune.
He might have known that they had to test their options.

    After all,
    He had!

ANGELS

People believed in angels then.
Not that they offered protection
as much as they made announcements,
a sort of communication system between God and man,
who sometimes wasn't all that delighted with what he heard!

Try to convince Anna and her husband
that Mary hadn't been fooling around!
Joseph wasn't thrilled either!
Must have taken a legion of angels
to do all that convincing!

So the angels sang their soothing songs,
and everyone settled back to wait.

Babies can move the stoniest hearts to belief!

The angels returned to sing more announcements
and bring a stormy world to its knees every year thereafter.

Why were there no angels for thirty-three years?

The next announcement was a whisper
breathed from the depths of an empty tomb.

MODERN ANGELS

Angels don't make dramatic appearances anymore!
They avoid groups, assume ordinary faces
and walk among us,
doing.

Your neighbor may be an angel.
Did he show up with his lawn mower
and mow,
when your back balled you into a fist of pain?

Your sister-in-law may be an angel.
She appeared in your kitchen with supper ready,
took charge of the children,
enfolded you in compassion when your father died.

The dry-cleaning lady may be an angel.
Remember the seam that mended itself,
the button no longer dangling,
the coat lining tacked up?

You may be an angel!
Those uncounted acts of kindness
thoughtlessly committed ...
Listen! the whisper of invisible wings!

UNFORGIVEN ...

they lie in icy dark,
unblinking,
staring upward to the wavering light.
Blind fish swim in the glassy black
caverns of their eyes,

weave among their ribs, their fingers.
A silty soup strains through their grinning teeth.

Their bones, entwined in sea grasses, remember
texture of silky hair,
the piney perfume of wooded shores,
the pitch and dance of the sturdy deck.

Cradled in the splintered bulkhead,
skeletons lie dreaming,
deaf to the mournful cries in the winds
shimmering silver,
fathoms above.

ALL WHO EVER LIVED

Everyone who was ever born is still on earth.
I swim through layers of time, of earth and stone,
and meet again my father and his father,
my grandmothers.

Howard and Florence lie together beneath one stone,
forty-nine years married.
Howard waited fourteen years for Florence to lie beside him.
They sleep together,
waking now and then into the memories of their children.

Next vault to the left,
Charlie and Bessie sleep, their bony fingers interlocked,
separated for thirty years.

Below the surface of oceans,
I see the mirthless grins
of lost mariners, of their ruthless captains.
Probing the cathedral walls of England
and into the tombs of my poet fathers,
I watch Keats turning and turning his Grecian Vase,
Shakespeare holding Yoric's skull.

Beside them lie the kings and queens:
the infamous and the obscure.
Henry VIII, his coffin overflowing with lopped noses
and ears of marble saints,
Ann Bolyn, sleeves hemmed to hide her sixth finger,
holds her head in her lap,
and, across the channel, Marie Antoinette
squirms in red velvet on a bed of petrified cake.

The immortal souls of Europe rest in hallowed tombs:
Pissarro and Monet, swathed in canvas,
untidy flowers scrambling on their graves,
Lautrec and Offenbach, silk garters and marabou
sifting among their bones,
Mozart, unfinished notes of his Requiem
stirring through the lime and mud in the paupers' graveyard,
and Sappho standing upright in her tomb,
unwilling to lie supine among men,
Michelangelo hugging marble in his bony arms,
Puccini wound in Japanese silk.

Everyone who ever lived is still on earth.
Adam Everyman lies unremembered,
hoes and swords and pens swarming
like worms among his bones.
Florence and Howard, Bessie and Charlie ...
Mr. and Mrs. Everyman ...
fragrance of farm and kitchen drifting into morning air,
wait ...
wait for me ...
and my brimming tomb.

SEPTEMBER 10, 2003

Two years ago today,
terrorists in the Middle East
were half the world around, so distant
they could be residing on another planet.

The next day,
they sliced the top off our world,
sent a snow storm of paper
dancing in super-heated air,
fluttering into drifts in the city canyons below.

In our homes and streets,
stalled in our morning patterns
on our way to work, to schools and shopping,
to cafes and dry cleaners,
we stopped, appalled,
unable to waken from the nightmare.

We watched as windows and walls melted,
as the contents of an entire city
crumbled into a giant crater:
copy machines, paper towels, purses and shoes,
chairs with jackets draped around their shoulders,
tables carrying crystal and silver,
desks trailing phone lines and computer cables,
dictionaries, pencils, and planners,
lamps and photographs and tissue boxes,
stairways shuffling like decks of cards,
people riding the brutal tide
into their common grave.

September tenth will never return.
We watch each other
and are watched.

UNCONDITIONAL

God has declared Himself parent
of all the peoples of the earth,
no matter what their beliefs.

Parents love their children,
unconditionally.
Sometimes they don't like
what they do, but
love them anyway.

Thus
God loves
  Adolph Hitler,
  Fidel Castro,
  Saddam Hussein,
  Osama bin Laden,
  Moamar Khadaffi,
  Jared,

  rapists, murderers,
  terrorists,
  me.

PROBLEMS BEING ACCEPTED

BREAKING BARRIERS

I place my car keys on the counter.
She drives the car to the service bay,
returns, saying,
    -Fifteen minutes.
I sit down to wait.

She fields a phone call,
explains the caller's car problems,
makes an appointment for repairs.
She pages through a catalogue,
dials, and gives detailed instructions
for equipment she needs.
A mechanic emerges from the service garage,
consults with her in a low voice,
and turns back, nodding.

I stand when she holds up my keys,
and, writing a check, ask,
    -Have you had problems
      being accepted in a man's world?
She laughs!
    -They all want to talk to my husband!

WINNIE

An elbow on the bar for balance,
she teeters on the high stool, crosses her legs,
and drags on her cigarette,
aiming the plume of smoke at the ceiling.

Her hand caresses the glass
as though the pleasure inside begins at her fingertips.
She tilts it down in a flaming gulp,
slides the glass back for more.

Another drag on the butt,
a raspy laugh, booted foot fidgeting.

The glass vanishes.
  -G'wan home, lady.
   Get some sleep.

   -Ya got no right!
   I got money same as ever'body else.

  -That's all!
  I'm gonna call a cab.

  -Neh' mind.
   I'm gonna get a bottle and have a party.
   Hey! who wans a pardy?

She pours off the stool onto melted legs,
slithers against a table.
  -How 'bout you 'n' me gettin' a bottle?

Words in a smog of tobacco and alcohol
wither onto the floor.
She lights a cigarette and sucks it hard.
Lifting her chin,
she tries to focus on the door.

PORTRAIT OF A MARRIAGE

She could see him from where she lay on the clay floor,
back to her, unconcerned.
Another contraction rolled forward from the small of her back,
harder than the last.

> Before the sun rose,
> she carried water from the stream
> and put in their meager clothes to soak.
> She ground corn
> and mixed and patted tortillas into flat cakes;
> he would be impatient to eat
> as soon as he came from their bed.
> She fed the children
> and sat them in the sunshine against the eastern wall
> to wait until their clothes,
> spread on stones in the yard, were dry.
>
> When her contractions could not be ignored,
> she sent the children down the dusty road to Maria,
> the oldest carrying the baby.

Her back arched in the storm of pain that racked her,
teeth clenched on a clean rag.
He sat smoking, tilted against the wall.
The baby surged downward and she strained,
alone.

At last, the birth accomplished,
she lay back exhausted, needing to tend her child.
She bathed him gently, wrapped him tightly,
called to her husband that they had a healthy son.

He went on smoking.

FIRST LADY

She perfected the distant smile,
chin up, shoulders back, imperious
illusion of control.

She knew what she had bought into
before the price was called.
The exchange was power,
prestige, setting standards, deciding
who should sit next to whom.

He oiled his way with charm, the veneer
covering lies and betrayal.

She kept up appearances,
learned the arts of investment and intrigue,
the evasive response.

As he struggles to maintain visibility,
impervious to disgrace,
she continues her calculated rise.
What will they call him...
        First Mate?
        First Gentleman?
        First Lord?

JARED'S MOTHER
- In January 2011, Jared Laughner killed a dozen people, injured many, and seriously wounded a congresswoman outside a mall in Phoenix, Arizona -

I do my marketing at midnight,
so as not to see neighbors -
or rapacious reporters!

They don't know what it is like,
the confusion,
humiliation.

His father hasn't gone to work,
lies on the davenport, staring,
not speaking.

At table, we sit across from each other,
swallowing stones,
drinking acid.

I brought home a beautiful baby boy,
held him, marveled,
nursed him.

Later, he loved Legos,
action figures,
and *Jack and the Beanstalk.*

He <u>was</u> different in teen years –
argumentative,
quick to anger,

but we thought it was
teen angst,
growing pains.

Please, leave me to my grief,
the irrevocable loss
of my baby boy.

MARILYN / NORMA JEAN – 1996

Norma Jean would have been seventy this summer;
    Marilyn would never have been seventy.

Norma Jean would have watched her grandchildren growing up,
would have circled around on the carrousel
and wondered with them at the macaque and cockatoo,
and the so-slow sloth at the zoo,
would have read tales of hapless princes
saved from rose gardens and reflection pools
by resourceful maidens.

    Marilyn turned her away, became the glamorous blonde
    envied and emulated by women,
    desired by men and movie producers.
    She married an author and a sports star,
    attracted a president and his brother.

The glorious smile and tight dresses and high heels
were never comfortable.
When Marilyn giggled on the subway grating,
Norma Jean pushed down her flying skirt.
Marilyn loved it all!
Why was Norma Jean so miserable?

    The charade was too much,
    and Marilyn couldn't keep explaining over and over
    to Norma Jean.
    They lay together on the bed
    and, holding each other,
    fell into final sleep.

GUEST POET

A benign, brotherly sort,
he reads his poems,
eliciting murmurs of appreciation
as his audience relates to his accessible,
homey imagery
and wonders why they hadn't thought that way before.

Afterward,
he receives their homage and signs his books
but is soon diverted by two comely college girls.

The local poet waits,
failing to attract his attention.
She no longer giggles.
She notices the wispy strands of hair
fanned out around his ears.

At last, he signs her book and
accepts the gift of her poem,
a response to one of his,
grudging the few seconds.
He says,
    -I suppose I must have it
      if you wrote about my poem!

I WISH YOU CHRISTMAS

CHURCH WINDOWS

Sapphire melts into silver hair;
amethyst dissolves upon a sleeve.
Jeweled light spills upon the hallowed air,
while people listen, sing, and pray,
and former generations whisper there.

Illumination spreads from music,
from the Word,
a holy Light diffusing into prayer.

Golden rays have haloed happy brides,
and misted mauve has baptized children at the font.
Men and women bowed with care
have bent their heads in hope of help
beneath the emerald angels, smiling there.

The tragedy of fire fused this family of Man
and blazed new dimensions into Light.
The windows stayed;
the congregation prayed.

Sapphire melting,
amethyst dissolving,
bathing worshippers in jeweled light,
the brilliant glow expands
upon their peaceful hands.

THE INNKEEPER'S GRANDDAUGHTER

All afternoon, I played in the stable.
Grandma lets me go down there when I visit
because I love the nooks and alcoves inside the big cave
and the smell of new hay and warm animals.

I asked Grandma for her broom
and, in a pile of straw, found a rake
so I could pretend it was my own little house.
After raking out the sour straw,
I swept until the ground was smooth and dry,
then spread fresh straw all around.

My doll, Samara, looked down from a ledge,
learning about proper housekeeping
and not to tease the sheep and cow,
who spoke softly now and then as I worked.

When all was neat and clean,
I set palm leaves and little gourd cups on a rock table,
moved Samara to her place,
and served our late-day bread-and-wine.
Then I laid her in a soft bed of wool and hay,
made for her in the manger.

When Grandma called,
I ran up to the inn for supper and sleep.

In the rose and gold of early morning,
I followed the shining path to the stable
to awaken Samara and found
the sweetest little real baby in her soft crib.

His mama and daddy were looking at him,
almost as amazed as I was,
while Samara watched from the ledge like a tiny angel
in the gold and white light of the new day.

PERILOUS JOURNEY

We heard the slow hoof beats
before we saw them, a man and his wife,
moving carefully along the rocky ravine.
I motioned to Barabbas to keep down,
to stay hidden by a huge boulder at the curve in the trail.

As we watched,
he glanced up at her, touched her hand.
We followed along the ridge above them,
waiting for an opportune moment to intercept them.
I could see a limp purse dangling from his belt,
and she carried a small bundle on the saddle blanket behind her.
These two would yield a meager haul at best,
the donkey perhaps their only asset.

We continued creeping along above them
as they kept a slow, steady pace.
Now and again, she would sing a soft song,
a psalm from the lyre of King David,
to encourage them both.

As shadows lengthened in the canyon,
they came to a trickling spring and stopped.
When he helped her down – oh gently –
we saw her condition and were amazed
that they should undertake their journey at such a time.

He spread the blanket on the ground
and helped her sit,
then filled a gourd with water.
She drank and leaned back against a rock – so tired.
He unrolled the bundle,
and they shared a poor meal of bread and dried fruit,
then lay down side by side covered with the blanket.
The donkey grazed patiently on dry grass.

Barabbas and I didn't speak
but, by mutual accord, made camp too
and kept watch through the night,
brightened by an amazing star rising in the eastern sky.
Distant wolves howled at the mystic light.
Just before dawn, she stirred and spoke to him.
He helped her onto the donkey, and they set forth.

Once we saw three highwaymen approaching
and waved them away.
If a thief claims a victim,
others respect his title to the spoils,
and we were there first.
An hour later, a mountain lion stalked their trail.
We spooked him by throwing rocks,
the sounds covered by the clop-clop of the donkey's hoofs.

Neither of us could explain
why we were guarding, not robbing, them.
There was a difference in their manner -
her patience, his concern for her –
but something else ...?
We are not religious men, but
I have to describe it as an aura of faith
that they were safe, protected.

At last, their path led to a slight rise,
and we knew that they would see Bethlehem in the distance.
To our astonishment, travelers converged from all directions
and were making camp in the fields around the village.
We would have plenty of victims to plunder
when they all returned homeward.

Barabbas and I watched
as the young couple plodded toward their journey's end,
the little donkey carrying them to their destiny ...

and ours,
when the star became a cross
and I hung there on my way to paradise.

THE CHILD

I have come from the inner sea,
swum the narrow channel,
and emerged onto cold earth
into life.

Soft eyes watch.
The young man looks stunned,
as if he had caught a bolt of lightning
in his hands.

Now I rest,
warmed by animal heat,
as this young woman murmurs songs of wonder
and caresses my moonlit hair.

I hear distant music,
strummed in the stars;
I breathe a fragrance of incense
drifting on winds from the east.

These are my magical hours.
The sheep and the cow speak in my tongue;
the donkey relates tales of those he has served,
of a time when he will carry a king.

In the far reaches of time,
I see men casting nets in the seas
and feel the pain of a hurting people.
I will give them hope and peace.

First I will forget.
I will learn the ways of this world,
and these mystical hours will evolve
into dream.

FORGOTTEN FATHER

His heart beats next to mine
as he sleeps in my arms,
head nestled in the hollow beneath my chin.
A miracle delivered into my hands,
he has struggled from his secret sea
and burst into the cold of earth.
Now he trusts me for warmth.

I will teach him what I know.
He will learn to lay strong foundations,
to build upon them straight and true.

I look down the years
and see him growing tall and taller,
leading men along a lake shore.
He will calm turbulent waters,
feed thousands of hungry souls.

Can I shelter him,
guide him,

and let him go?

A GRANDMOTHER'S MEDITATION

He snuggles into my shoulder,
sucking and chirping in his sleep,
while I rock, humming soft songs into his light-lit hair.
      Praise the Lord that they returned unharmed!

She wouldn't listen! She seemed to have a mission!
      How I worried!
He promised to take care of her,
took his donkey to help her over rocky trails.
      I took every jolt with her.

I could have eased her confinement.
My heart ached at her account of the crowded city,
the poor shelter where she gave birth,
warmed only by the animals stabled there.

      Sleep, little one!
      He smiles in his dreams.

They tell of visitors sent by angels,
Wise Men led by a star.
She has exotic gifts they could not have bought.

The whole year has been full of mystery
and so hard for her father and me!
      We were angry,
          bewildered when she told us of an "Angel from God."
      She had never lied!
      And then Joseph disclaimed her,
      said the child was not his!
      Her father was furious!

We were amazed when Joseph returned to wed her,
stunned by his story about angels ...
events beyond our understanding.
      We knelt with them to pray and praise,
      and peace returned to our hearts.

      There, there, dear one! Sleep!
      His tiny fingers tangle in my hair.

They escaped from Herod's police
lived for months with townsfolk who sheltered them.
> Praise God for generous hearts!

Now, Mary cares for her home and her son,
visits at the well with her neighbors.
Joseph builds cabinets and coffins and cradles
as if the events of this year were commonplace.

> I hold my grandchild,
> begin to tell him the tales he must know,
> sing songs into his glowing hair,
> and watch his star moving westward.

LEAH'S CHRISTMAS

No lights except the twinkling tree
and silky reflections in the tall windows.

She steps toward the tree, arms raised,
and sings,
words created out of her need
and joy in that moment.
The song leads her feet into dance.
She dances deliberately,
her arms lifting,
hands turning like opening flowers.

Her song spins into the room,
offered to this surprising magic of Christmas.
Her tiny feet know the rhythm of a tree
hung with treasures.

She is two.

CHRISTMAS WISHES

I wish you Christmas
    in frigid dark of February
        when light and land are locked in ice and snow,
        that you may warm by spiced cup and fire glow.

I wish you Christmas
    during rain-time in April,
        when sun-fire hides in cloud-draped gloom,
        that your crocus-candles will burst into bloom.

I wish you Christmas
    in sun-burned August,
        when heat crumbles earth and dries your dreams,
        that you may breathe cool fragrance of evergreen.

I wish you Christmas
    in crisping days of October,
        when light begins to fail and brisk winds tease,
        that crimson and gold will illuminate your trees.

I wish you Christmas
    in the stress of your days
        when your mood is blue
        that love-gifts will open their blessings to you.

PUBLISHING CREDITS AND AWARDS

A POTENTIALLY POETIC PLACE

VIOLETS AND RAIN
    2001: *PENINSULA POETS*, Fall Issue, p. 13 – Published by The Poetry Society of Michigan / 4th prize, Nature Category, Annual Contest

JUST DAWN
    1984: *PLUM PUDDING* – 10th Anniversary Anthology, Published by The Poets' Workshop, Saginaw, Michigan; Pen-Dec Press Marysville, Michigan
    1990: *ANTHOLOGY NINETEEN-NINETY,* p. 75 – Published by The Poetry Society of Michigan

SOUNDS OF SUMMER REMEMBERED
    1984: *PENINSULA POETS*, Fourth Quarter / 1st Prize, Lyric Category, Annual Contest – Published by The Poetry Society of Michigan

SUMMER HEAT
    1996: *PENINSULA POETS*, Spring Issue / Annual Contest, 1st Prize, Nature Category – Published by The Poetry Society of Michigan

GULF WIND
    1980: *THE LITERARY PLUM,* Vol. 5, No. 2, p. 8 – Published by The Saginaw Public Libraries

OCEAN
    2010: *MICHIGAN! LYRICAL REFLECTIONS OF THE GREAT LAKES,* p. 80 – Anthology, Published by The Poetry Society of Michigan

ROCKY MOUNTAIN TIME
    1976: *POEMS FOR THE BICENTENNIAL MICHIGAN,* 1976, p. 97 – Published by Delta College; Gerald L. Hall and Jeremy W. Kilar, Editors

OCTOBER IN THE WOODS
    1980: *PENINSULA POETS*, Fourth Quarter, p. 13 – Published by The Poetry Society of Michigan
    1981: *THE LITERARY PLUM*, Vol. 6, No. 1, p. 5 – Published by The Saginaw Public Libraries

THE BRINK OF WINTER
    1984: *PENINSULA POETS*, Fourth Quarter, p. 5 – Published by The Poetry Society of Michigan

WINTER BEACH
    1993: *PENINSULA POETS*, Fall Issue – Published by The Poetry Society of Michigan

THE WALLS WHISPER OUR SECRETS

FATHER, IN MEMORIAM
    1989: *PENINSULA POETS*, Spring Issue, p. 8 – Published by The Poetry Society of Michigan /1st Prize, Loss Category, Annual Contest

THE BLUE SPRUCE CAFÉ
    1999: *PENINSULA POETS*, Spring Issue, p. 11 – Published by The Poetry Society of Michigan / 2nd Prize, Loss Category, Annual Contest

FLAT TIRE, FLUSHING, L.I., Circa 1909
    2000: *SING THEN I MUST*, p. 98 – Anthology, Published by The Poetry Society of Michigan

BEACH WONDERS
    1977: *THE LITERARY PLUM*, p. 38, Contest Issue – Published by The Saginaw Public Libraries / 2nd Prize, Adult poetry
    1990: *PENINSULA POETS*, Spring Issue, p. 35 – Published by The Poetry Society of Michigan

BRET ANDREW – February 5, 2003
    2003: *PENINSULA POETS*, p. 68, October / Contest Issue – Published by The Poetry Society of Michigan / 1st Prize, Family Category
    2010: *CELEBRATING POETS OVER 70*, p. 1 – Published by McMaster University, Hamilton, Ontario; Marianne Forsyth Vespry and Ellen Ryan, Editors

THE WINDING TRAIL OF EXPLORERS' DREAMS

GRAND CANYON
    2012: *PENINSULA POETS*, p. 2, Fall Contest Issue – Published by The Poetry Society of Michigan /1st Prize, Margo Lagattuta Award

HIGHWAY CALIFORNIA
    1995: *HEART SONGS*, p. 76 – Anthology, Published by The Poetry Society of Michigan

DENALI / McKINLEY
    2000: Poetry Society of Michigan Annual Contest: 3rd Honorable Mention, Nature Category – not published

PYRAMIDS OF TEOTIHUACAN
    2000: *VISIONES DIFERENTES, II, An Anthology of Poetry*, Published by The Saginaw Art Museum, Compiled by The River Junction Poets; Edited by Judith Kerman and Marion Tincknell

OAXACANA
    2011: Honorable Mention, Abbie Copps Contest, Olivet College – not published

CATHEDRAL CONCERT, OAXACA
    2006: *PENINSULA POETS*, October Contest Issue, p. 61 Published by The Poetry Society of Michigan / 2nd Prize, Premier Category

GOURNIA, CRETE
    2005: *I HEAR THE SONG ... AND IT WELLS IN ME*, p. 211 – Anthology, Published by The Poetry Society of Michigan

RAINBOWS FROM MY PRISMS

MY FRIEND, MY LOVER, MY CHILD
    1984: *PLUM PUDDING* – 10th Anniversary Anthology, Published by The Poets' Workshop; Pen-Dec Press, Marysville, Michigan

RENDEZVOUS
    1992: *3RD WEDNESDAY, 1991-2* – Anthology, 3rd Wednesday Poetry Workshop, Published by Saginaw Valley State University, Judith Kerman, Editor

JUST DESSERT
    2007: *IN OTHER WORDS*, p. 5 – Cedar Crest College Literary Magazine, Vol. 9, No. 2 – Allentown, PA.

SECRETS THEY DO NOT SHARE

"ALL THE MONKEYS AREN'T IN THE ZOO"
    1984: Poetry Society of Michigan Annual Contest: Honorable Mention, Children's Category – not published

NICHOLAS
    2009: *MEOW POETRY, Fun, Fabulous, Feline Verse*, p. 56 – Outskirts Press, Denver, CO; Jeffrey Winke, Editor

PUSSY CAT, PUSSY CAT, WHERE HAVE YOU BEEN?
    2001: *PENINSULA POETS*, Fall Issue, p. 37 – Published by The Poetry Society of Michigan

HAYLEY IN MIDDLE AGE
    2006: *PENINSULA POETS*, April Issue, p. 41 – Published by The Poetry Society of Michigan

MALLARD
    1988: *PENINSULA POETS*, Fall Issue, p. 30 – Published by The Poetry Society of Michigan – Read on his Sunday morning radio program, WJR, by Ted Strasser

THE MAGICAL SHIMMER

GLASS SHOES
    2005: *PENINSULA POETS*, October / Contest Issue, p. 52 – Published by The Poetry Society of Michigan – 2nd Prize, Humor Category

THE LEGEND OF KYLA, HAWK WOMAN
    1996: *THE MacGUFFIN, Special Issue, Vol. XIII, No II,* "Myth and *Magik*," p. 4 – Published by Schoolcraft College, Livonia, Michigan; Arthur J. Lindenberg, Editor – (Nominated for a Pushcart Prize)

BRASSY RHYTHM
    1993: *PENINSULA POETS*, Spring Issue – Published by The Poetry Society of Michigan

PROBLEMS BEING ACCEPTED

WINNIE
    2000: Poetry Society of Michigan Annual Contest, 1st Honorable Mention, Narrative Category – not published

PORTRAIT OF A MARRIAGE
    1992: *3RD WEDNESDAY, 1991-92, Poems from the 3rd Wednesday Poetry Workshop*, Published by Saginaw Valley State University; Judith Kerman, Editor
    1994: *THE GARFIELD LAKE REVIEW* – Published by Olivet College / Honorable Mention, Abbie Copps Contest
    1999: *VISIONES DIFERENTES*, p. 6 – An Anthology of Poetry Published by The Saginaw Art Museum, Compiled by The River Junction Poets; Carol Scott, Marion Tincknell, Judith Kerman , Editors

I WISH YOU CHRISTMAS

CHURCH WINDOWS
    1982: Set to music for solo voice by Page Long, Minister of Music, First Congregational Church, Saginaw, Michigan

ABOUT THE AUTHOR

MARION FRAHM TINCKNELL, born in 1928 in Flushing, Long Island, was educated at Friends Academy in Locust Valley, Long Island, and at Cedar Crest College in Allentown, Pennsylvania, where she received her BA degree in 1951 with a major in French and English Literature. She has had her poetry published in nine anthologies and in many small magazines, including *The MacGuffin*, a publication of Schoolcraft College; her poem, "The Legend of Kyla, Hawk Woman" in the special issue, *Superstition, Myth, and Magik*, was nominated for a Pushcart Prize in 1997. She has presented poetry performances and workshops in schools, churches, libraries, and gatherings of adults for more than thirty-five years. She was an Artist-in-the-Schools for the Bay Arts Council for seven years, visiting elementary schools all over Bay County (Michigan). She participated for thirteen years in the Summer Magic Program, a summer art and activity day camp for underprivileged children at a local Church. She was secretary of The Poetry Society of Michigan from 1988 until 2002 and has been a member of The River Junction Poets since its beginning in 1974. In recent years, she has taken classes in watermedia painting. She lives in Saginaw, Michigan with her husband, Les. They have four children and fourteen grandchildren.

www.ingramcontent.com/pod-product-compliance
Lightning Source LLC
Chambersburg PA
CBHW032135040426
42449CB00005B/246